THE GOOD HABITS PLAYBOOK

The Art of Playfully Changing Your Habits

Ralph Sterling

Contents

Copyrights	1
Prologue: Embarking on a Joyful Journey of Transformation	2
1. The Power of Play: Why Habits Matter More Than You Think	9
2. Brain Games: How Habits Sculpt Your Mind	17
3. Fun with Flaws: Overcoming Bad Habits	25
4. Detective Work: Identifying Bad Habits with a Smile	33
5. The Habit Transformation Game: A Step-by-Step Guide	41
6. The Joy of Habitual Revolution: Making Change Fun	49
7. Engaging Friends and Family in Your Playful Habit Change	58
8. Conclusion: Triggering Massive Change with Small Steps	66

Copyright © 2024 by Ralph Sterling

All rights reserved.

No portion of this book may be reproduced in any form without written permission from the publisher or author, except as permitted by U.S. copyright law.

This publication is designed to provide accurate and authoritative information in regard to the subject matter covered. It is sold with the understanding that neither the author nor the publisher is engaged in rendering legal, investment, accounting or other professional services. While the publisher and author have used their best efforts in preparing this book, they make no representations or warranties with respect to the accuracy or completeness of the contents of this book and specifically disclaim any implied warranties of merchantability or fitness for a particular purpose. No warranty may be created or extended by sales representatives or written sales materials. The advice and strategies contained herein may not be suitable for your situation. You should consult with a professional when appropriate. Neither the publisher nor the author shall be liable for any loss of profit or any other commercial damages, including but not limited to special, incidental, consequential, personal, or other damages.

Prologue: Embarking on a Joyful Journey of Transformation

In the heart of life's complexity and the challenges we all inevitably face, there lies a profound truth: transformation, although arduous, is within reach. This book is not about quick fixes or magical solutions. Rather, it's a testament to the hard-earned wisdom that comes from a life spent in pursuit of meaningful change.

The Unseen Battle

My journey, much like yours, has been filled with battles against habits that, at first, seemed innocuous. But as time passed, these habits became architects of a reality I hadn't consciously chosen. Breaking free from this unchosen reality was like trying to escape a labyrinth I had unwittingly built around myself. The process was arduous, often frustrating. There were victories, setbacks, and moments of profound self-doubt. But every struggle, every fall, taught me something invaluable.

The Realization

It was during one of these moments, on a particularly trying day, that an epiphany struck me. The struggle wasn't just about eliminating bad habits; it was about understanding them. It was about recognizing that each habit, good or bad, was a response to something deeper – a need, a fear, a desire. The key wasn't in battling these habits head-on but in understanding and redirecting the underlying currents that gave rise to them.

A New Approach

This realization led me to a new approach. Instead of seeing the process of change as a war, I began to view it as a journey – a series of steps, each taking me closer to the person I wanted to become. This perspective didn't make the journey easy, but it made it meaningful. And in that meaning, I found the strength to continue, even when the path was steep and obscured.

The Power of Insight

What surprised me the most was the power of insight. Each habit, once understood, lost much of its hold over me. This wasn't an overnight transformation but a gradual awakening. As I began to see the patterns, the triggers, and the rewards that each habit brought, I gained the power to reshape them.

Small Changes, Big Impact

Another surprising revelation was the power of small changes. In my earlier attempts at transformation, I had aimed for sweeping reforms, only to be overwhelmed and discouraged by their weight. But when I shifted my focus to smaller, more manageable changes, the impact was profound. These small victories created a momentum of their own, propelling me forward.

Embracing the Journey

As you embark on your own journey of transformation, I want to share these insights with you. This book is a distillation of the lessons I've learned – a guide to help you navigate the complexities of habit change with a clearer understanding and a renewed sense of purpose.

Embracing Playfulness

After years of battling my habits, I discovered a transformative truth: the journey of change, although challenging, need not be joyless. This realization came to me not in a moment of triumph but during a time of reflection, after yet another seemingly failed attempt to alter a deep-seated habit. The epiphany was simple yet profound – the process of change could be as enriching as the outcome.

The Role of Playfulness

I began to weave a sense of playfulness into my efforts. This was not about trivializing the struggle or denying the effort involved. Rather, it was about approaching each day with a sense of curiosity and openness. It was about finding joy in the small, incremental steps of progress and learning to laugh at the inevitable missteps along the way.

Reimagining the Journey

Incorporating playfulness transformed my journey. Tasks that had once seemed daunting became puzzles to be solved. Challenges became opportunities for creativity and growth. This shift in perspective didn't erase the difficulties, but it made them more bearable, even enjoyable at times.

The Power of Curiosity

Curiosity became my compass. I started to question why certain habits were so ingrained and what joy or comfort they provided. This inquiry led to surprising discoveries about myself and my motivations. It also opened up new pathways for change that were previously hidden by the rigid mindset of seeing habits as enemies to be conquered.

Learning to Laugh

Laughter, I found, was a powerful ally. It lightened the weight of failure and diffused the frustration that often accompanies the process of change. By learning to laugh at myself, I was able to view setbacks as part of the journey rather than signs of defeat.

Small Joys, Big Differences

The concept of finding joy in the small things brought a new dimension to the habit-changing process. Celebrating the tiny victories and acknowledging the incremental progress made the overall goal seem more attainable. It was no longer about a distant, daunting change but about the enjoyable journey towards it.

Embracing the Unpredictable

Playfulness also meant embracing unpredictability. Change is rarely linear, and habits don't always respond to our efforts in the way we expect. By accepting this unpredictability as part of the process, I learned to adapt and respond with flexibility rather than frustration.

A New Way of Seeing

This approach brought a new lightness to my life. It wasn't that the habits themselves had changed overnight, but my perception of them had. I saw them as part of a larger tapestry of self-improvement, each thread integral to the overall picture.

The Impact of a Playful Approach

What surprised me the most was the impact this approach had on my overall well-being. Stress and anxiety, which had often accompanied my previous attempts at habit change, were significantly reduced. I found myself more resilient, more capable of facing the ups and downs of the journey.

Sharing the Playful Path

As you embark on your own journey of habit transformation, I invite you to embrace playfulness. Allow yourself to experiment, to be curious, and to find joy in the process. Remember that change is not just about reaching a destination but about the growth and learning that happens along the way.

Setting the Stage for Transformation

In my years of striving for personal growth, I've learned that the journey of transforming habits begins long before the first tangible steps are taken. It starts in the quiet, often overlooked moments of introspection and decision. This part of the journey, though less visible, is crucial. It sets the stage for everything that follows.

The Moment of Decision

My journey has taught me that true transformation starts with a clear, unequivocal decision. This isn't a fleeting wish or a half-hearted resolution but a deep, unwavering commitment to change. It's a moment where you stand at the crossroads of your current self and the self you aspire to be, and you choose the path of growth.

Understanding the 'Why'

The foundation of any lasting change is understanding the 'why' behind it. Why do you want to change? What drives you towards this transformation? For me, the answers to these questions were not immediately apparent. It took deep reflection to unearth the genuine motivations that could sustain me through the challenges ahead.

The Role of Self-Awareness

Self-awareness is a powerful ally in setting the stage for transformation. It involves being brutally honest with yourself about your strengths and weaknesses, your habits, and the impact they have on your life. This self-awareness doesn't come easily. It requires courage to confront aspects of yourself that you may have been avoiding.

Crafting a Vision

A clear vision of who you want to become acts as a guiding star on your journey of change. My vision was not just about shedding undesired habits but about embracing a new way of being. It was a detailed, vivid picture of my best self – the person I knew I could be if I stayed true to my path.

Embracing the Complexity of Change

Change is complex. It's not a linear path but a winding road with ups and downs. Recognizing this complexity is essential. It prepares you for the journey ahead and arms you with the resilience to face the inevitable challenges.

The Importance of a Support System

No transformation occurs in isolation. Along my journey, I learned the value of a strong support system. This includes not just friends and family but also mentors, peers, and sometimes professionals. Their support, advice, and encouragement can be a lifeline during difficult times.

Setting Realistic Goals

In my experience, setting realistic, achievable goals is crucial. These goals act as milestones, giving structure to your journey and a sense of accomplishment as you reach them. They should be challenging yet attainable, pushing you out of your comfort zone while still being within reach.

The Power of Small Steps

One of the most surprising insights for me was the power of small, consistent steps. Transformation doesn't happen overnight. It's the result of daily choices and actions, no matter how small. These small steps accumulate over time, leading to profound changes.

Cultivating Patience and Persistence

Patience and persistence are virtues that cannot be overstated in the journey of habit transformation. There were times when progress seemed painfully slow or nonexistent.

But it was persistence, the ability to keep going in the face of adversity, and patience, the capacity to wait for the results, that eventually led to success.

Learning from the Past

Your past experiences, both successes and failures, are invaluable teachers. In my journey, reflecting on past attempts at change, understanding what worked and what didn't, helped me to refine my approach and avoid repeating the same mistakes.

The Journey Begins

As you stand on the brink of your own transformation, remember that the path ahead is as much about the journey as it is about the destination. Each step, each decision, each day is a part of the tapestry of change you are weaving. You have the power to shape your journey, to learn from it, and to emerge transformed.

1. The Power of Play: Why Habits Matter More Than You Think

1.1 Joy in the Small Things

In the grand tapestry of habit transformation, it's the small threads – the seemingly insignificant daily actions and choices – that create the most enduring and vivid patterns. This subchapter explores how finding joy in these small things can be a powerful catalyst for profound change.

The Misconception of Monumental Change

My journey, like those of many others, started with the misconception that change had to be monumental to be meaningful. This belief often led to overwhelming goals and unrealistic expectations. However, the truth I discovered was quite different. Real, lasting change often begins with the smallest of steps, steps that are easily overlooked in the pursuit of grand transformation.

The Power of Micro-Habits

Micro-habits, those tiny, almost effortless actions, can quietly revolutionize our lives. A small change, like waking up ten minutes earlier to meditate or writing a single gratitude note each day, might seem trivial in isolation. Yet, when these micro-habits are consistently practiced, they compound into significant transformations.

Celebrating the Tiny Triumphs

One key to finding joy in the small things is to celebrate every tiny triumph. In my experience, acknowledging these minute successes generates a sense of accomplishment and motivates further action. It wasn't the grand gestures that kept me on track; it was the recognition and celebration of the small, daily victories.

The Ripple Effect

The ripple effect of small changes is often surprising. A simple habit, like decluttering a small area of your home each day, can lead to a more organized and peaceful environment, which in turn can enhance mental clarity and reduce stress. These seemingly minor actions can set off a cascade of positive changes in other areas of life.

Consistency Over Intensity

In the realm of habit change, consistency trumps intensity every time. It's not the intensity of the effort that matters most, but the regularity with which you engage in the new habit. A small habit, done consistently, can lead to more significant change than sporadic efforts at larger goals.

The Mindset Shift

One of the most profound insights I gained was the need for a mindset shift. Instead of focusing solely on the end goal, I learned to find joy and value in the process itself. This shift in perspective transformed mundane tasks into enjoyable rituals.

Small Steps, Big Picture

While celebrating the small steps, it's also important to keep the big picture in view. Each small habit, each minor change, is a step towards a larger goal. Recognizing this connection between the micro and the macro provides a sense of purpose and direction.

Overcoming Resistance

Small steps are also key in overcoming resistance. It's often easier to talk ourselves into taking a small, manageable action than a larger, more daunting one. By focusing on these smaller steps, I found it easier to maintain momentum and avoid the paralysis that often accompanies the prospect of significant change.

The Habit of Noticing

Cultivating the habit of noticing the small joys and successes in everyday life can change one's outlook significantly. This practice of mindfulness, of being present and acknowledging the little pleasures, enriches the journey of habit change and life itself.

The Foundation for Larger Change

Finally, I realized that these small habits were not just steps towards change; they were the foundation upon which larger transformations were built. As these micro-habits became ingrained, they created a solid base from which to tackle more significant challenges.

1.2 Playing the Long Game: Lifelong Habits

In our journey through life, the habits we cultivate and carry with us are more than mere actions; they are the threads that weave the fabric of our existence. This subchapter delves into the concept of lifelong habits – those enduring practices that shape our lives in profound ways, often without us even realizing it.

The Concept of Lifelong Habits

Lifelong habits are those deeply ingrained practices that we perform almost unconsciously, yet they govern much of our daily lives. They're the routines we adhere to from youth into old age, the rituals that provide comfort and structure, and the consistent behaviors that define our identity over time.

The Formation of Lifelong Habits

The roots of these habits often trace back to our earliest years, influenced by family, culture, and personal experiences. However, the true power in these habits lies in their evolution – how they adapt and grow with us over time. It's a process of continuous refinement, learning, and adjustment.

The Impact of Lifelong Habits on Our Lives

The most profound insight I gained over the years is the silent yet significant impact these habits have on the course of our lives. Lifelong habits can shape our health, happiness, relationships, and even our success. They are like the rudder of a ship, subtly steering us through the waters of life, often without us being aware of their guiding presence.

The Challenge of Changing Lifelong Habits

Modifying a lifelong habit can be one of the most challenging aspects of personal transformation. These habits are deeply rooted in our psyche, fortified by years, sometimes decades, of repetition. Yet, it is their very depth and strength that make changing them so impactful.

Embracing the Process of Change

The process of altering these ingrained habits requires patience, persistence, and a deep understanding of oneself. It involves unraveling layers of behavior and often confronting uncomfortable truths. But it's within this process that we find opportunities for profound growth and self-discovery.

The Role of Reflection

Reflection is a crucial tool in understanding and reshaping lifelong habits. It involves looking back over the years to identify the habits that have served us well and those that have held us back. This introspection is not about dwelling on the past but about learning from it to create a better future.

Creating New Lifelong Habits

As we journey through life, there's also the opportunity to cultivate new lifelong habits. This process is about more than just adopting a new behavior; it's about embedding it into the very fabric of our daily existence, making it a part of who we are and who we aspire to become.

The Importance of Consistency

Consistency is the cornerstone of developing and maintaining lifelong habits. It's not the grand, sweeping changes that forge these enduring practices, but the small, consistent actions repeated day after day, year after year.

Lifelong Habits and Identity

Over time, I've come to understand that our lifelong habits are a reflection of our deepest values and beliefs. They are an expression of our identity and, in many ways, a legacy we leave behind. Changing or creating these habits, then, is not just about altering actions but about evolving as individuals.

The Journey Forward

As you contemplate the lifelong habits that have shaped your journey so far, and those you wish to cultivate for the road ahead, remember that this is a game played over decades, not days. It's a commitment to continuous growth and a testament to the enduring power of our actions over time.

1.3 Habit Stories: Real-Life Transformations

In the journey of life, each of us is a mosaic of habits, some that hold us back and others that propel us forward. This subchapter is dedicated to the stories of real-life transformations, tales that underscore the profound impact of habits on our lives. Through these narratives, we find not only inspiration but also practical wisdom that can guide our own paths of change.

The Power of a Single Habit Change

One of the most striking stories I encountered was that of Sarah, a middle-aged office worker whose life was transformed by a single habit change. Plagued by chronic stress and its accompanying health issues, Sarah decided to start walking for 30 minutes every day. This simple habit didn't just improve her physical health; it became a keystone change that rippled through every aspect of her life. It boosted her mental health, improved her relationships, and even led to a career change. Sarah's story is a testament to how one small habit, consistently practiced, can have a domino effect on our entire lives.

Breaking Free from Negative Habits

Another compelling tale comes from David, who struggled with a smoking addiction for over a decade. His journey to freedom was not just about quitting a harmful habit but about understanding the underlying reasons for his addiction. Through self-reflection and support, David learned to cope with stress and anxiety in healthier ways. His story is a powerful reminder that breaking free from negative habits often requires us to confront deeper emotional and psychological challenges.

The Habit of Mindfulness

Linda, a high school teacher, found transformation through the habit of mindfulness. Overwhelmed by the demands of her job and personal life, she began practicing mindfulness meditation. This practice didn't just help her manage stress; it changed how she interacted with her students, colleagues, and family. Linda's story highlights how cultivating internal habits, like mindfulness, can profoundly affect our external world.

From Chaos to Order

Mike's transformation centered around the habit of organization. A self-described 'chaotic' person, Mike's disorganized lifestyle was affecting his personal and professional life. The change began with the simple habit of dedicating ten minutes each morning to planning his day. This small step led to more significant organizational habits that transformed his life from chaos to order, enhancing his productivity and overall well-being.

The Journey of Self-Discovery

Emma's story is one of self-discovery through the habit of journaling. Facing a personal crisis, she began to write daily as a form of self-expression and reflection. This habit became a tool for understanding her thoughts and emotions, leading to greater self-awareness and ultimately, a clearer sense of direction in her life.

The Ripple Effect of Positive Habits

John's story demonstrates the ripple effect of positive habits on others. By adopting healthier eating and exercise habits, John not only improved his own health but also inspired his family to adopt a healthier lifestyle. His story illustrates how our habits can influence those around us, creating a positive cycle of change within our communities.

Overcoming the Impossible

Lisa's journey speaks to overcoming what seems impossible. Battling a lifelong struggle with obesity, she felt trapped in a cycle of failed diets and exercise regimes. However, by shifting her focus to building sustainable habits rather than seeking quick fixes, Lisa achieved what she once thought was impossible. Her transformation is a powerful reminder that lasting change often requires a shift in mindset and approach.

The Habit of Continuous Learning

Tom's story is about the habit of continuous learning. Faced with a rapidly changing job market, Tom committed to learning something new every day, whether it was a skill related to his job or a personal interest. This habit not only kept him relevant in his career but also ignited a passion for lifelong learning.

2. Brain Games: How Habits Sculpt Your Mind

2.1 The Neuroscience of Play and Habit Formation

In the intricate dance of habit formation and change, our brains play a pivotal role. This subchapter delves into the fascinating interplay between neuroscience, play, and habit formation, offering insights from a life spent unraveling the mysteries of our mind's workings.

Understanding the Brain's Plasticity

At the heart of habit formation is the brain's remarkable ability to change – its plasticity. Neuroplasticity, the brain's ability to reorganize itself by forming new neural connections throughout life, is fundamental to our ability to develop new habits and discard old ones. This plasticity is not static; it can be nurtured and enhanced through our actions and experiences.

The Role of Neurotransmitters in Habit Formation

Neurotransmitters, the brain's chemical messengers, play a crucial role in habit formation. Dopamine, often referred to as the 'feel-good' neurotransmitter, is particularly significant.

It's released in response to rewarding activities, reinforcing the behaviors that led to the reward. This dopamine-driven feedback loop is a core component of habit formation, encouraging the repetition of rewarding behaviors.

The Habit Loop: Cue, Routine, Reward

Understanding the habit loop – cue, routine, reward – is crucial in understanding how habits are formed and maintained. A cue triggers a behavior (routine), which is then followed by a reward. This cycle, over time, becomes automatic, creating a neural pathway that makes the behavior more likely to be repeated.

The Impact of Play on the Brain

Play, in its various forms, has a profound impact on the brain. It stimulates the release of neurotransmitters like dopamine, endorphins, and serotonin, which not only make us feel good but also enhance our brain's plasticity. This stimulation makes play an effective, albeit often overlooked, tool in habit formation and change.

Harnessing Neuroplasticity for Habit Change

The key to changing habits lies in leveraging the brain's neuroplasticity. By introducing new routines and ensuring they are followed by a reward, we can create new neural pathways. Over time, these pathways can become stronger than those of the old habits, effectively rewiring our brain to adopt new behaviors.

The Power of Repetition and Consistency

Repetition and consistency are critical in habit formation. Each time a new behavior is repeated, the neural pathways associated with that behavior are strengthened. This process, known as synaptic pruning, helps the brain to become more efficient, gradually making the new behavior more automatic. Breaking established habits poses a challenge due to the strength of the neural pathways formed over years of repetition. However, understanding that these pathways can be rewired through consistent new behaviors provides a roadmap for successful habit change.

The Role of Mindfulness in Habit Formation

Mindfulness can play a significant role in habit formation and change. By increasing our awareness of our thoughts, feelings, and behaviors, mindfulness allows us to recognize the cues and rewards that drive our habits, providing us with the opportunity to consciously alter them.

The Impact of Stress on Habits

Stress can significantly impact our habits, often leading to the reinforcement of negative behaviors. Understanding the neurobiological link between stress and habit formation can be crucial in developing strategies to manage stress and prevent it from derailing our habit change efforts.

Towards a Neuroscience-Informed Approach to Habits

A deeper understanding of the neuroscience behind habit formation and change can empower us to approach our habits more effectively. By leveraging the principles of neuroplasticity, reward systems, and mindful awareness, we can develop more sustainable and effective strategies for personal transformation.

2.2 Rewiring for Joy: The Plasticity of the Brain

The human brain, a marvel of nature, possesses a remarkable trait – plasticity. This ability of the brain to rewire and adapt itself is a beacon of hope and a tool of transformation for anyone seeking to alter their habits. In this subchapter, we explore how understanding and harnessing this plasticity can lead to a joyful and fulfilling journey of habit change.

The Foundation of Neuroplasticity

Neuroplasticity is the brain's capacity to form new neural connections and pathways in response to experience. This capability challenges the once-held belief that the adult brain is static. On my own journey of habit change, embracing the concept of neuroplasticity was a game-changer. It meant that no habit was too ingrained, no pattern too fixed to be altered.

The Role of Experience in Shaping the Brain

Our experiences, both positive and negative, play a crucial role in shaping our brain. Each action, thought, and emotion creates electrical activity in the brain, strengthening certain neural pathways while weakening others. This understanding highlights the importance of mindful action and thought patterns in rewiring our brain for positive habit formation.

The Impact of Positive Habits on Brain Plasticity

Engaging in positive habits not only benefits our well-being but also enhances our brain's plasticity. Activities that stimulate the brain, such as learning a new skill, practicing mindfulness, or engaging in physical exercise, can lead to the development of new neural pathways, making the brain more adaptable and resilient.

The Science of Habit Replacement

One of the most effective ways to change a habit is to replace it with a new, positive one. This process takes advantage of the brain's plasticity. By consistently practicing a new behavior in response to a familiar cue, we can forge new neural pathways, eventually making the new behavior more automatic than the old one.

The Role of Dopamine in Reinforcing Positive Habits

Dopamine, the neurotransmitter associated with pleasure and reward, plays a significant role in habit formation. Engaging in activities that we find enjoyable and rewarding releases dopamine, reinforcing the habit. This is why incorporating joy and personal interest into new habits can make them more sustainable. Old habits are underpinned by well-established neural pathways, making them challenging to break. However, with consistent effort and the strategic application of new habits, these old pathways can become less dominant. It's a process that requires time, patience, and perseverance.

Stress, Brain Plasticity, and Habits

Stress can be a major obstacle in rewiring the brain, as it can negatively impact neuroplasticity. Managing stress through relaxation techniques, exercise, and adequate sleep is crucial in maintaining the brain's ability to form new habits.

The Power of Visualization

Visualization is a powerful tool in the realm of neuroplasticity. By vividly imagining performing a new habit, we can stimulate the same neural networks as if we were actually performing the action. This practice can help in strengthening the neural pathways associated with the new habit.

The Lifelong Journey of Brain Adaptation

Neuroplasticity is not just a tool for short-term habit change but a lifelong journey. As we age, maintaining a brain that is adaptable and resilient becomes increasingly important. Engaging in lifelong learning and new experiences is key to keeping our brains healthy and pliable.

Practical Steps to Leverage Brain Plasticity

Understanding neuroplasticity is just the beginning. The real magic happens when we apply this knowledge in practical ways to change our habits and, consequently, our lives. This requires a combination of knowledge, strategy, and most importantly, action.

2.3 Mindful Play: Using Habits to Enhance Mental Health

In the landscape of habit formation and mental health, mindfulness stands out as a beacon, guiding us toward greater self-awareness and well-being. This subchapter explores the intersection of habits and mindfulness, emphasizing how the deliberate incorporation of mindful practices can profoundly impact our mental health.

The Intersection of Habits and Mindfulness

The journey of habit change is intimately linked with mindfulness – the practice of being present and fully engaged with whatever we're doing, free from distraction or judgment. Mindfulness, when woven into our daily habits, has the power to transform not just individual actions but our entire perspective on life.

Understanding Mindfulness

Mindfulness is often misunderstood as a complex or esoteric practice. In reality, it is about being fully present in the moment, aware of our thoughts, feelings, and sensations without resistance or judgment. This simple yet profound practice can be integrated into any habit, enhancing both the habit and our mental state.

The Role of Mindful Habits in Mental Health

Mindful habits are particularly effective in managing stress, anxiety, and depression. By cultivating awareness of our thoughts and reactions, we can break free from the automatic responses that often exacerbate these conditions. Mindful habits create a space between stimulus and response, allowing us to choose how we react.

Habitual Mindfulness in Daily Life

Incorporating mindfulness into daily life doesn't require extra time or special circumstances. It can be as simple as paying full attention while brushing your teeth, eating mindfully, or taking a few deep, conscious breaths during your day. These practices, though small, can have a significant cumulative effect on mental well-being.

The Power of Breath

One of the most accessible and powerful mindful habits is focused breathing. The act of taking slow, deliberate breaths is a form of grounding that can calm the mind, reduce stress, and bring us back to the present moment. This habit can be a refuge in times of turmoil and a source of clarity in decision-making.

Mindful Movement

Integrating mindfulness into physical activity – whether it's yoga, walking, or more vigorous exercise – enhances the benefits of both the physical activity and the mindfulness practice. This combination can lead to improved mood, reduced anxiety, and a heightened sense of well-being.

The Benefits of a Mindful Morning Routine

Starting the day with a mindful routine sets a tone of calm and intention that can carry through the entire day. Whether it's a few minutes of meditation, a mindful cup of tea, or simply sitting quietly to set intentions for the day, these practices can significantly impact our mental state and approach to our habits.

Cultivating Gratitude

The habit of gratitude is a powerful form of mindfulness. By regularly acknowledging and appreciating the positive aspects of life, we shift our focus from what we lack to what we have. This shift can have profound effects on our mental health, fostering a sense of contentment and well-being.

Mindfulness in Interpersonal Habits

Mindfulness can also transform our interpersonal habits. By being fully present in our interactions with others, we cultivate deeper connections and more meaningful relationships. This practice involves active listening, empathy, and being conscious of our words and actions.

Overcoming Mental Health Challenges Through Mindful Habits

For those struggling with mental health challenges, incorporating mindful habits can be a valuable part of a comprehensive wellness strategy. It's important to note that mindfulness is not a cure-all, but it is a tool that can support better mental health when used in conjunction with other therapies and treatment. The journey of integrating mindful habits is a lifelong one, with each step offering an opportunity for growth and self-discovery. As we cultivate these habits, we enhance not only our mental health but also our overall quality of life.

3. Fun with Flaws: Overcoming Bad Habits

3.1 Identifying and Laughing at Our Flaws

In the quest to overcome bad habits, the first step is often the hardest yet most crucial: identifying and acknowledging our flaws. This subchapter explores the journey of recognizing our imperfections, not with self-criticism or despair, but with a light-hearted acceptance that paves the way for genuine change.

The Art of Self-Reflection

Self-reflection is an indispensable tool in identifying our flaws. It involves stepping back and observing our behaviors, thoughts, and emotions with an objective lens. Through my own journey, I learned that this process, while potentially uncomfortable, is rich with insights. It's not about judging ourselves harshly but about understanding ourselves better.

The Role of Humor in Self-Acceptance

Integrating humor into the process of acknowledging our flaws can be surprisingly liberating. Laughter brings lightness to our self-reflection, allowing us to see our imperfections not as damning faults but as facets of our human experience. It's about learning to laugh at our quirks and follies, diffusing the heaviness that often accompanies self-criticism.

Identifying Habitual Patterns

Our flaws often manifest as habitual patterns that we repeat unconsciously. These might include procrastination, impulsive reactions, or negative self-talk. By identifying these patterns, we begin to understand the 'what' and 'why' of our behaviors, which is the first step towards change.

Embracing Our Imperfections

Embracing our imperfections does not mean resigning ourselves to them; rather, it means acknowledging them without self-judgment. This acceptance is crucial as it shifts our mindset from one of self-defeat to one of self-improvement.

The Power of Self-Compassion

Self-compassion is a powerful ally in dealing with our flaws. It involves treating ourselves with the same kindness and understanding that we would offer to a good friend. This approach fosters a supportive internal environment for change, as opposed to the stifling atmosphere created by self-criticism.

The Role of Feedback

Feedback from trusted friends, family, or colleagues can be invaluable in identifying our flaws. Often, others can see aspects of our behavior that we are blind to. Accepting this feedback with grace and humor can open our eyes to what needs to change.

Recognizing Triggers

Many bad habits are triggered by specific situations or emotional states. Identifying these triggers is a crucial step in habit change. It involves not just recognizing the external triggers but also understanding the internal emotional responses that precede the habit.

Learning from Past Attempts

Reflecting on past attempts to change bad habits can provide valuable insights. What strategies worked? What led to relapse? This reflection is not about dwelling on past failures but about learning from them.

Setting the Stage for Change

Once we've identified and embraced our flaws with humor and self-compassion, we're ready to set the stage for change. This involves creating a realistic, step-by-step plan to alter the habits that stem from our flaws, equipped with the insights gained from our self-reflection.

Conclusion: A Journey of Self-Discovery

Identifying and laughing at our flaws is more than just the first step in overcoming bad habits; it's a journey of self-discovery. It requires honesty, courage, and a sense of humor. But the rewards – increased self-awareness, personal growth, and the eventual transformation of habits – are immeasurable.

3.2 Strategies for Playful Change

While confronting and changing deep-seated habits is often a challenging journey, integrating strategies that add an element of enjoyment and lightness can make the process more engaging and sustainable. This subchapter delves into various strategies that infuse a sense of playfulness into the serious task of habit change, drawn from a lifetime of experience and learning.

Embracing the Power of Gamification

Gamification, the process of adding game-like elements to everyday activities, can be a powerful tool in habit change. By turning habit change into a game – complete with challenges, rewards, and progress tracking – we can make the process more engaging and fun. This approach not only adds an element of playfulness but also leverages the brain's reward system to reinforce new habits.

Setting Up Personal Challenges

One effective strategy is to set up personal challenges. These challenges should be specific, measurable, and time-bound. For example, committing to a 30-day challenge to exercise daily, meditate, or practice a new skill. The key is to view these challenges not as chores but as opportunities for personal growth and enjoyment.

Creating Reward Systems

Establishing a reward system can significantly enhance the process of habit change. The rewards can be simple – a favorite treat, an evening of relaxation, or a small purchase. The anticipation of a reward can increase motivation and make the journey more enjoyable.

Using Visualization Techniques

Visualization is a powerful tool in habit formation. Imagining yourself successfully engaging in a new habit can be both fun and motivating. This practice not only prepares the mind for change but also adds an element of playfulness to the process.

Building a Supportive Community

Having a supportive community can add a social and fun aspect to habit change. Whether it's a group of friends, family members, or an online community, sharing your journey, celebrating each other's successes, and learning from each other can make the process more enjoyable and less isolating.

Incorporating Playful Reminders

Incorporating playful reminders in your environment can help keep you motivated and focused on your habit change goals. These can be humorous sticky notes, creative vision boards, or fun alarms and apps that remind you of your new habits in an engaging way.

Mixing Up Routines

Variety is not only the spice of life but also a key component in habit change. Mixing up your routines can prevent boredom and keep the process interesting. For instance, if your goal is to exercise more, try different forms of exercise to keep it engaging and fun.

Learning Through Play

Approaching new habits with a mindset of learning and exploration can add a sense of playfulness to the process. Viewing each attempt, success or failure, as a learning experience makes the journey more about exploration and less about rigid achievement.

Celebrating Small Wins

Acknowledging and celebrating small victories is crucial in keeping the journey light-hearted and rewarding. These celebrations don't have to be grand; sometimes, simply taking a moment to acknowledge your progress can be incredibly uplifting.

Reflecting with Humor

Reflect on your progress with a sense of humor. Not every attempt at habit change will be successful, and that's okay. Learning to laugh at your setbacks reduces their emotional weight and allows you to approach them with a more positive mindset.

Conclusion: A Playful Path to Transformation

Integrating these strategies can transform the often daunting task of habit change into a more enjoyable and sustainable journey. By infusing playfulness into the process, we can shift our perspective on habit change from one of mere discipline to one of engaging self-improvement.

3.3 Celebrating Small Victories

In the arduous journey of habit change, recognizing and celebrating small victories can be a powerful motivator. This subchapter focuses on the importance of acknowledging even the smallest progress, a practice that has been a cornerstone in my own journey of transformation and can be profoundly impactful for anyone on a similar path.

The Importance of Small Victories

Small victories are the incremental achievements we make as we work towards a larger goal. They may seem minor when viewed in isolation, but collectively, they form the backbone of successful habit change. Each small victory is a step forward, a proof of progress, and a building block for bigger achievements.

The Psychology Behind Celebrating Small Wins

From a psychological perspective, celebrating small victories has a significant impact. It triggers the release of dopamine, a neurotransmitter associated with feelings of pleasure and satisfaction. This release reinforces the positive behavior, making it more likely to be repeated. Over time, this reinforcement helps in solidifying the new habit.

Setting Milestones

Setting clear, achievable milestones along the journey of habit change can provide opportunities for celebration. These milestones should be realistic and tailored to your personal goals. For instance, if your goal is to improve fitness, a milestone might be completing a certain number of workouts or reaching a specific fitness level.

Reflecting on Progress

Regular reflection on progress is essential in recognizing small victories. Keeping a journal, using apps to track progress, or simply taking time to reflect at the end of each day can help in acknowledging and celebrating these wins. It's about being mindful of each step forward, no matter how small.

Sharing Your Success

Sharing your progress with friends, family, or a support group can amplify the joy of small victories. Not only does it provide a sense of accountability, but it also allows others to celebrate with you, providing encouragement and motivation.

The Role of Self-Compassion

In the process of celebrating small victories, self-compassion plays a significant role. It's important to treat yourself kindly and acknowledge that progress, not perfection, is the goal. This attitude helps in maintaining a positive and resilient mindset, even when facing setbacks.

Creating Personal Rituals

Creating personal rituals around celebrating victories can add a sense of fun and significance to the achievement. It could be as simple as a small treat, a moment of relaxation, or a special activity that you enjoy. These rituals become markers of progress and sources of joy in the habit change journey.

Learning from Each Victory

Each small victory holds valuable lessons. Reflecting on what worked, what didn't, and what can be improved helps in refining your approach to habit change. It's not just about celebrating the outcome but also about understanding the process that led to the success.

Building Momentum

Celebrating small victories helps in building momentum. Each success builds confidence and reinforces the belief that change is possible. This momentum is crucial in overcoming the inevitable challenges and setbacks that accompany any journey of change.

The Cumulative Effect of Small Victories

Over time, the cumulative effect of these small victories can be astonishing. They add up, leading to significant transformations that may have seemed impossible at the outset. It's a process of gradual evolution, where each small step contributes to a larger, more profound change.

Conclusion: A Journey Marked by Celebrations

In sum, celebrating small victories is about more than just acknowledging progress; it's about creating a journey marked by positive reinforcement, learning, and joy. It's a crucial strategy in the toolkit of anyone seeking to change their habits and transform their life.

4. Detective Work: Identifying Bad Habits with a Smile

4.1 The Habit Sleuth: Becoming a Detective in Your Life

In the quest to identify and change bad habits, adopting the role of a detective in your own life can be an enlightening experience. This subchapter explores how to become a 'Habit Sleuth', investigating your own behaviors, patterns, and triggers to uncover the underlying habits that need change.

Embracing the Role of a Habit Sleuth

Becoming a Habit Sleuth means adopting a mindset of curiosity and inquiry about your own life. It's about carefully observing your daily routines, interactions, and reactions to uncover the habits that are quietly influencing your life. This process requires patience, attention to detail, and a non-judgmental approach. The first step in this detective work is observation. Start by tracking your daily activities, noting not only what you do but also when you do it and how you feel while doing it. This can be done through journaling, using apps, or simply taking mental notes. The goal is to gather as much data as possible about your habitual behaviors.

Identifying Patterns

Once you have collected enough data, the next step is to identify patterns. Look for recurring behaviors, especially those that are automatic or seem to happen without much thought. These could be as simple as reaching for a snack when stressed or as complex as patterns of negative thinking in certain situations.

Understanding Triggers

Every habit has a trigger – an event, situation, or feeling that initiates the habitual behavior. Identifying these triggers is crucial in understanding your habits. Pay attention to what happens right before you engage in a bad habit. Is it a particular time of day, a feeling of boredom, or a response to stress?

Analyzing Rewards

Every habit also has a reward – the reason you keep doing it. It might be a feeling of relief, a sense of escape, or a temporary pleasure. Understanding the reward that your bad habit provides is key to changing it, as it helps in finding healthier ways to achieve the same reward.

The Role of Environment

Your environment plays a significant role in your habits. Investigate how your surroundings – the people, places, and things around you – might be contributing to your bad habits. Sometimes, small changes in your environment can have a big impact on your behavior.

Reflecting on Past Attempts

Reflect on your past attempts to change these habits. What worked? What didn't? Why did you revert back? This reflection can provide valuable insights and help you avoid repeating the same mistakes.

Gathering Evidence

As you gather evidence about your habits, it becomes easier to see the bigger picture. This process can lead to surprising discoveries about why you do what you do and provide a clear direction for change.

Consulting with Others

Sometimes, an outside perspective can be incredibly helpful. Don't hesitate to discuss your findings with a trusted friend, family member, or counselor. They might offer insights that you hadn't considered.

Developing a Plan of Action

With all the evidence in hand, the next step is to develop a plan of action. This plan should be based on the insights you've gained about your triggers, rewards, and the role of your environment in your habits.

The Journey of Change

Remember, identifying your bad habits is just the beginning of the journey. Changing them requires consistent effort and patience. But with the insights gained from your detective work, you are better equipped to make lasting changes.

Conclusion: A Path to Self-Discovery

Becoming a Habit Sleuth is more than just a strategy for habit change; it's a path to deeper self-discovery and understanding. It's about uncovering the hidden aspects of your behavior and taking control of the habits that shape your life.

4.2 Clues and Cues: Recognizing Habit Patterns

The journey to transform our habits begins with a keen understanding of the clues and cues that trigger them. This subchapter delves into the art of recognizing habit patterns, an essential skill I've honed over years of introspection and change. It's about becoming aware of the subtle signals that precede our habitual actions and learning to respond to them differently.

The Subtlety of Habit Cues

Habit cues are often subtle and can be easily overlooked. They can be environmental, such as a place or time of day, emotional, like a feeling of stress or boredom, or even social, triggered by the presence of certain people. Recognizing these cues requires a heightened sense of awareness and a willingness to closely examine our daily routines.

The Habit Loop: Cue, Routine, Reward

Understanding the habit loop – cue, routine, reward – is essential in recognizing and changing habits. The cue triggers the routine (the habit itself), which is then followed by a reward (the reason we repeat the habit). Identifying each component of this loop is crucial in understanding how to change it.

Journaling for Awareness

Journaling can be an effective tool for recognizing habit patterns. By documenting your daily activities and feelings, you can begin to see patterns emerge. Over time, this record will reveal the cues that lead to certain habits and the rewards that keep them in place.

Mindfulness in Action

Mindfulness practice is another powerful tool for recognizing habit patterns. It involves paying close attention to your present actions and feelings without judgment. This heightened awareness can bring clarity to the habitual behaviors that often go unnoticed.

Environmental Triggers

Our environment can have a profound impact on our habits. Certain locations, times of day, or contexts can trigger habitual behaviors. By changing or avoiding these environmental triggers, you can reduce the occurrence of the habit.

Emotional Cues

Emotions are powerful drivers of habits. Feelings like anxiety, sadness, or even happiness can trigger habitual responses. Recognizing these emotional cues is the first step in learning how to manage them in healthier ways.

The Influence of Others

The people around us can also cue our habits. Whether it's a smoking break with colleagues or a family tradition of unhealthy eating, social cues can be powerful. Recognizing these influences can help in creating strategies to counteract them.

The Power of Routines

Routines themselves can be cues for habits. A morning routine, for instance, might include unhealthy habits like skipping breakfast or checking emails immediately after waking up. Altering these routines can be a key strategy in habit change.

The Reward System

Rewards are what make habits stick. Sometimes the reward is obvious, like the pleasure of a sweet treat. Other times, it's more subtle, like the emotional relief from stress eating. Understanding the reward you get from a habit is crucial in finding healthier alternatives that provide similar satisfaction.

Using Technology to Track Patterns

There are numerous apps and tools available to help track your habits and their cues. These can be helpful in identifying patterns you might not be aware of and providing data to inform your habit change strategies.

Reflection and Adaptation

Regular reflection on the patterns you've identified is key. This can involve revisiting your journal, adjusting your mindfulness practices, or tweaking your routines. The goal is to remain adaptable and responsive to the insights you gain.

Conclusion: Mastering the Art of Recognition

Recognizing habit patterns is an art that requires practice, patience, and persistence. By mastering this skill, you lay the groundwork for meaningful and lasting change in your habits and, ultimately, your life.

4.3 The Aha! Moment: Realizing the Need for Change

In every journey of transformation, there comes a pivotal moment of realization – an 'Aha! Moment' – when the need for change becomes clear. This subchapter explores these profound moments of insight, drawn from a life rich with experiences of confronting and altering deeply ingrained habits.

The Nature of the Aha! Moment

An Aha! Moment in the context of habit change is a flash of clarity where the impact of a bad habit becomes undeniably clear. It often feels like a sudden revelation, but it's usually the result of a gradual process of gathering insights about one's behaviors and their consequences.

Building Up to the Moment

These moments don't occur in a vacuum. They are often preceded by a period of growing awareness and discomfort about a particular habit. It's like the slow rise of water in a pot – the temperature increases gradually until it reaches a boiling point.

Triggers of the Aha! Moment

Different factors can trigger these moments. It could be a comment from a loved one, a particularly jarring consequence of a habit, or an accumulation of negative outcomes. For me, it was a combination of health concerns and realizing the impact of my habits on those around me.

Recognizing the Moment

Recognizing an Aha! Moment requires a level of self-awareness. It involves being open to introspection and honest self-evaluation. It's about listening to that inner voice that's been nudging you towards realization and accepting the truth it reveals.

Embracing the Moment

Once you experience this moment of realization, embracing it is crucial. While it might be tempting to retreat into denial, embracing the Aha! Moment is the first step towards meaningful change. It's acknowledging that the way you've been doing things needs to be altered.

The Role of Emotions

Emotions play a significant role in these moments. They can range from guilt and frustration to hope and determination. Embracing these emotions, even the uncomfortable ones, is part of processing the realization and moving forward. Following an Aha! Moment, the power of decision comes into play. It's a crossroads where you choose whether to act on your realization or ignore it. This decision is critical as it sets the course for your journey of habit change.

Planning After the Realization

Post-realization, the next step is to start planning for change. This involves setting goals, identifying resources, and preparing for the challenges ahead. It's about turning the insight of the Aha! Moment into actionable steps.

Seeking Support

Seeking support after experiencing an Aha! Moment can be invaluable. Whether it's from friends, family, support groups, or professionals, having others to share your journey with can provide encouragement and accountability.

Reflecting on the Journey

Reflecting on the journey that led to the Aha! Moment can provide further insights and motivation. It's about understanding the journey that brought you here and using those lessons to propel you forward.

The Continuous Journey

Finally, it's important to recognize that the journey of habit change doesn't end with the Aha! Moment. It's a continuous process of learning, growing, and evolving. The Aha! Moment is just the beginning of a new chapter.

5. The Habit Transformation Game: A Step-by-Step Guide

5.1 Setting Up the Board: Laying the Foundations

Embarking on a journey to change habits is akin to setting up a board for an intricate and rewarding game. This subchapter, drawn from a lifetime of navigating the challenging yet enriching process of habit change, lays out the foundational steps necessary to begin this transformative journey effectively.

Understanding the Game of Habit Change

Habit change can be conceptualized as a strategic game where the ultimate prize is personal growth and improved well-being. Like any game, understanding its rules, objectives, and strategies is essential. The first rule in this game is that change is gradual and requires patience and persistence.

Assessing Your Current Position

The starting point of any habit change is a clear and honest assessment of your current habits. This involves identifying both good and bad habits and understanding their impact on your life. It's like taking stock of the pieces on the board before making a move.

Clarifying Your Vision

Having a clear vision of what you want to achieve is crucial. This vision will guide your actions and decisions throughout the journey. It should be specific, realistic, and aligned with your values and long-term goals.

Setting Specific Goals

Once your vision is clear, the next step is to set specific, measurable, achievable, relevant, and time-bound (SMART) goals. These goals should be small enough to be attainable but significant enough to drive meaningful change.

Understanding the Psychology of Habits

A fundamental part of laying the foundation is understanding how habits work. This includes learning about the habit loop (cue, routine, reward), the role of the brain in forming and breaking habits, and the psychological factors that influence habit change.

Building Self-Awareness

Self-awareness is a critical tool in habit change. It involves being conscious of your thoughts, feelings, actions, and their triggers. Developing self-awareness can be achieved through practices like mindfulness, journaling, and reflection.

Creating a Supportive Environment

Your environment plays a significant role in your habit change journey. This includes your physical surroundings, the people you interact with, and your daily routines. Altering your environment to support your new habits can significantly increase your chances of success.

Developing a Plan

With a clear understanding of your goals and the environment, the next step is to develop a detailed plan. This plan should outline the steps you need to take, resources you might require, and strategies to overcome potential obstacles.

Equipping Yourself with Tools and Resources

Various tools and resources can aid your habit change journey. These might include apps to track your progress, books for guidance and inspiration, or tools for time management and organization. Choose tools that resonate with you and fit into your lifestyle.

Preparing for Challenges

Anticipating challenges and preparing for them is a vital part of the foundation. This includes identifying potential triggers for old habits, planning for how to deal with setbacks, and developing coping strategies.

Commitment to the Journey

Finally, the most critical part of laying the foundation is committing to the journey. This commitment means being prepared for hard work, being open to learning and growth, and staying the course even when progress seems slow. With the board set and the foundations in place, you are now ready to start the game of habit transformation. Remember, this game is not won overnight. It's a journey of continuous effort, learning, and adaptation.

5.2 Rules of the Game: Structuring Your Habit Changes

In the game of habit transformation, structuring your changes effectively is as crucial as knowing the rules of any game. This subchapter is dedicated to outlining the 'rules of the game' – a framework that guides the structuring of habit changes. Drawing from years of experience and observation, these rules are designed to make the process of habit change more manageable, effective, and sustainable.

Understanding the Rules

The 'rules' in the context of habit change are not strict laws but rather guidelines that help structure the process of change. These rules are based on psychological principles, practical wisdom, and an understanding of human behavior.

Rule 1: Start Small

The first rule is to start small. Overwhelming yourself with drastic changes often leads to failure. Instead, focus on making small, incremental changes that gradually lead to larger transformations. This approach reduces resistance and makes the process more manageable.

Rule 2: Consistency Over Intensity

Consistency is more important than intensity. Regularly practicing a new habit, no matter how small, is key to making it stick. It's about building a new routine that becomes a natural part of your day-to-day life.

Rule 3: Focus on One Habit at a Time

Trying to change multiple habits simultaneously often leads to spreading yourself too thin. Focus on one habit change at a time. This concentrated effort allows you to channel your energy and resources effectively, increasing the chances of success.

Rule 4: Understand the Why

Understanding the reason behind wanting to change a habit is crucial. This understanding provides motivation and a sense of purpose, especially during challenging times. It's about connecting the habit change to your larger life goals and values.

Rule 5: Set Clear, Measurable Goals

Vague goals lead to vague results. Set clear, specific, and measurable goals for your habit change. This clarity helps in tracking progress and provides a clear target to aim for.

Rule 6: Create a Supportive Environment

Your environment should support your habit change. This might mean altering your physical surroundings, spending time with people who support your goals, or even avoiding certain triggers that lead to the bad habit.

Rule 7: Use Positive Reinforcement

Positive reinforcement is a powerful tool. Reward yourself for making progress. These rewards don't have to be grand; they just need to provide a sense of achievement and encouragement.

Rule 8: Be Prepared for Setbacks

Setbacks are a natural part of the habit change process. Be prepared for them and treat them as learning opportunities. It's not about avoiding setbacks but about how you respond to them.

Rule 9: Monitor and Adjust

Regularly monitor your progress and be willing to adjust your strategies. Flexibility is key in responding to challenges and changing circumstances.

Rule 10: Practice Self-Compassion

Be kind to yourself throughout the process. Change is hard, and self-criticism can be demotivating. Practice self-compassion and remind yourself of the progress you've made, even if it's small.

The Application of the Rules

Applying these rules is not a linear process. It involves constant evaluation, adjustment, and persistence. Each individual's journey will be different, and these rules should be adapted to fit personal circumstances and goals.

Building a Structured Plan

With these rules in mind, the next step is to build a structured plan for your habit change. This plan should outline the specific steps you'll take, the resources you'll use, and the timeline you aim to follow.

Tracking Progress

Tracking progress is essential in this structured approach. Use tools like journals, apps, or even a simple calendar to mark your progress. This tracking not only provides a sense of accomplishment but also helps in identifying patterns and areas for improvement.

Seeking Feedback

Regular feedback, either from yourself or from others, can provide valuable insights. It helps in assessing the effectiveness of your approach and making necessary adjustments.

The Role of Reflection

Reflecting on your journey is a crucial part of the process. It involves looking back at the challenges faced, the successes achieved, and the lessons learned. This reflection helps in gaining a deeper understanding of yourself and your habit change process.

By understanding and applying these rules, the process of habit change becomes more structured and less daunting. It's about playing the game smartly, using a well-thought-out strategy that aligns with your life and goals.

5.3 Playing to Win: Maintaining Momentum

In the game of habit transformation, maintaining momentum is critical to ensuring long-term success. This subchapter, drawn from a wealth of personal experience and observation, focuses on strategies to keep the momentum going, even when the initial excitement of habit change begins to wane.

The Challenge of Sustaining Momentum

Maintaining momentum in habit change is often more challenging than starting the change itself. The initial enthusiasm can fade, and the reality of sustained effort sets in. Understanding this challenge is the first step in overcoming it.

Building a Routine

Consistency is key in maintaining momentum. Building a routine around the new habit helps embed it into your daily life. This routine should be practical, achievable, and aligned with your daily schedule and lifestyle.

Setting Short-Term Goals

While long-term goals provide direction, short-term goals offer immediate milestones to aim for. These should be specific, achievable, and time-bound, serving as checkpoints that keep you motivated and focused.

Tracking Progress

Tracking your progress is vital in maintaining momentum. Whether it's through journaling, apps, or a visual progress tracker, seeing how far you've come can be a powerful motivator. Regularly review your progress to appreciate your achievements and understand areas needing improvement.

Celebrating Milestones

Celebrating milestones, no matter how small, reinforces positive behavior and keeps the journey enjoyable. These celebrations don't have to be grand; sometimes, acknowledging your progress to yourself or sharing it with a friend can be a powerful reward.

Adapting to Change

Flexibility is crucial in maintaining momentum. Be prepared to adapt your strategies as circumstances change. This adaptive approach helps in overcoming obstacles without losing sight of your overall goal.

Overcoming Plateaus

Encountering plateaus, where progress seems to stall, is normal. During these times, it's important to reassess your strategies, seek new sources of inspiration, or even take a short break to recharge if needed.

The Role of Social Support

Having a support system can provide the encouragement needed to maintain momentum. This could be a community of like-minded individuals, a mentor, friends, or family. Sharing your journey with others can provide accountability and motivation.

Dealing with Relapse

Relapse, or falling back into old habits, can happen. It's important not to view relapse as failure but as a part of the learning process. Analyze what led to the relapse, learn from it, and use this knowledge to strengthen your approach.

Keeping the End Goal in Sight

Always keep your end goal in sight. Remind yourself why you started this journey and the benefits that the new habit brings to your life. This long-term perspective helps in navigating through tough times.

Staying Inspired

Staying inspired is crucial. Regularly engage with sources of inspiration, whether it's reading, podcasts, seminars, or personal reflection. Inspiration can reignite your motivation and provide new ideas to enhance your journey. Finally, embrace the journey. Habit transformation is not just about the destination but also about the growth and learning along the way. Recognize that every step, even the setbacks, is a part of your progress.

6. The Joy of Habitual Revolution: Making Change Fun

6.1 Gameifying Your Goals

In the challenging yet rewarding journey of habit change, transforming the process into a game – gamifying your goals – can be a remarkably effective strategy. This subchapter draws from a rich reservoir of experience and knowledge, illustrating how infusing game elements into habit formation can make the journey more engaging, enjoyable, and successful.

Understanding Gamification

Gamification is the art of applying game principles and design elements in non-game contexts. It's about making an otherwise mundane process stimulating and fun. This approach leverages the human psychological response to gaming – such as reward-seeking, competition, and achievement – to motivate and sustain behavioral change.

The Psychology Behind Gamification

The psychological basis of gamification lies in its ability to tap into our intrinsic motivators. Elements like points, badges, and leaderboards trigger the release of dopamine, a neurotransmitter linked to feelings of pleasure and satisfaction, thereby reinforcing the desired behaviors.

Setting the Stage for Gameified Habit Change

1. **Define Clear Objectives**: Just like a game has clear objectives, define specific, achievable goals for your habit change. These should be concrete and measurable, providing a clear target to aim for.

2. **Establish Rules**: Set rules that govern your habit change process. These could include daily routines, specific limitations, or conditions under which you perform the new habit. Rules help in maintaining structure and discipline.

3. **Incorporate Challenges and Levels**: Divide your journey into levels or stages, each presenting its own set of challenges. Overcoming each challenge or moving up a level can provide a sense of accomplishment and progression.

4. **Create a Reward System**: Rewards are vital in gamification. Establish a system where you earn points, badges, or other rewards for meeting certain milestones or maintaining consistency. These rewards should be meaningful and motivating.

Leveraging Technology

1. **Use Apps and Tools**: Numerous apps and digital tools are designed to gamify habit change. These tools can track progress, provide reminders, and offer rewards, making the process more interactive and enjoyable.

2. **Virtual Communities**: Engage with online communities or platforms where you can share your progress, compete with others, and seek support. This social aspect can add a layer of accountability and encouragement.

Making It Personal and Fun

1. **Personalize Your Game**: Tailor the game elements to suit your personal preferences and interests. Whether it's themed rewards or custom challenges, personalization can significantly enhance engagement and enjoyment.

2. **Incorporate Variety and Creativity**: Keep the game dynamic by regularly introducing new challenges or changing the rules slightly. This variety can prevent boredom and keep you engaged.

Tracking and Reflecting

1. **Monitor Your Progress**: Regularly track your progress and reflect on your performance. This could involve reviewing your point scores, badges earned, or levels achieved. Use this information to adjust your strategies and keep improving.

2. **Celebrating Milestones**: Celebrate milestones in your game. Whether it's reaching a new level or achieving a streak, acknowledging these achievements can provide a sense of pride and accomplishment.

Overcoming Obstacles

1. **Dealing with Setbacks**: Like any game, expect challenges and setbacks. Develop strategies to deal with these effectively, such as loss of points or redoing a level. This approach can help in maintaining resilience and determination.

2. **Adjusting the Difficulty**: Be flexible in adjusting the difficulty of your challenges. If a particular level or stage is too hard or easy, modify it to ensure it remains challenging yet achievable.

Long-Term Engagement

1. **Sustaining Interest**: To keep the game interesting in the long term, introduce periodic updates or changes. This could involve setting new goals, adding new rewards, or even playing with others.

2. **Reflecting on the Journey**: Regularly take time to reflect on your journey and the progress you've made. Recognize how the gamification of your habit change has influenced your behavior and mindset.

A Transformative Game

Gamifying your habit change process is not just about making it fun; it's about harnessing your natural responses to gaming for a greater purpose. It's a creative and effective strategy to transform your habits and, by extension, your life.

6.2 Rewards and Revelry: Celebrating Progress

The journey of habit change, while challenging, should also be a journey of joy and celebration. This subchapter explores the critical role of rewards and revelry in acknowledging and celebrating the progress made in altering habits. Drawing from a wealth of personal experiences and insights, it emphasizes how integrating celebration into the habit change process can significantly enhance motivation and the overall experience.

Understanding the Role of Rewards and the Art of Rewarding Yourself

Rewards play a pivotal role in habit formation and change. They serve as positive reinforcement, a psychological principle that rewards a behavior, making it more likely to be repeated. Rewards tap into our basic neurological pathways, releasing dopamine, a neurotransmitter associated with pleasure and motivation. Choosing the right rewards is an art. They should be meaningful, attainable, and aligned with your goals. The reward system can be simple, like treating yourself to a favorite meal or activity for consistently practicing a new habit for a week.

Structuring Rewards

Structuring rewards effectively is key to sustaining motivation. It involves setting clear criteria for what constitutes earning a reward. This structure prevents the reward system from becoming arbitrary and ensures it reinforces the desired behavior.

Small Rewards for Small Wins

Small victories deserve recognition too. Acknowledge the achievement of minor milestones with small rewards. This could be as simple as an extra hour of relaxation for a day of successful habit practice. These small rewards keep the momentum going and provide constant motivation.

Celebrating Milestones

Significant milestones call for bigger celebrations. Completing a month of a new exercise regimen or a year without a bad habit are substantial achievements and should be treated as such. These celebrations can be shared with friends and family, making them more meaningful.

Reward Variety

Variety in rewards helps in maintaining interest and excitement. Rotate between different types of rewards to keep the reinforcement fresh and engaging. This variety caters to different aspects of your personality and needs, keeping the reward system dynamic.

Non-Material Rewards

Not all rewards need to be material or external. Internal rewards like self-recognition, pride in your achievements, and the enjoyment of the new habit itself can be incredibly powerful. Cultivating appreciation for these internal rewards is crucial for long-term habit change.

Making Celebrations a Habit

Incorporate celebrations into your routine. This could mean setting aside time at the end of each week to reflect on and celebrate your progress. Making celebration a habit ensures that it becomes a natural part of your habit change journey.

Sharing Success

Sharing your successes with others can amplify the joy of your achievements. Whether it's with a support group, friends, or family, sharing creates a sense of community and shared joy. It also provides a sense of accountability and encouragement.

Reflective Revelry

Celebration should also be a time for reflection. Reflect on what these achievements mean to you, the challenges you've overcome, and how you've grown. This reflective process provides deeper satisfaction and insights into your personal journey.

Balancing Rewards with Goals

While celebrating progress is important, it's crucial to balance rewards with your overall goals. Rewards should not contradict or undermine your habit change efforts. For instance, if your goal is to eat healthily, rewarding yourself with junk food might be counterproductive.

The Psychology of Celebration

Celebrating progress taps into the psychology of positive reinforcement, but it also acknowledges the human need for joy and satisfaction. It's a recognition that the journey itself should be as rewarding as the destination. Cultivate a culture of celebration in your life. This means not only celebrating your own progress but also recognizing and celebrating the achievements of others. This culture creates a positive environment conducive to growth and change.

The Ripple Effect of Celebrating Progress

Celebrating your progress can have a ripple effect on your overall outlook and approach to life. It instills a positive mindset, encourages a focus on growth, and can influence other areas of your life, leading to a more holistic and fulfilled existence.

Revelry as a Revolution

In conclusion, integrating rewards and revelry into the habit change process is not just about acknowledging progress; it's about transforming the journey into a fulfilling and enjoyable experience. It's a revolution in how we approach change – one that embraces joy, satisfaction, and a deep appreciation for the journey.

6.3 Keeping the Game Fresh: Adapting and Evolving

Habit change, much like a game, can lose its appeal if it becomes monotonous or fails to evolve with our changing needs. This subchapter, drawn from extensive life experience in the realm of self-improvement, focuses on strategies for keeping the habit change process fresh, adaptable, and continually evolving.

The Importance of Adaptability

Change is constant, and our approach to habit transformation should be no different. The ability to adapt and evolve your strategies is crucial to maintaining engagement and effectiveness. Rigidity can lead to stagnation, making the habit change process feel like a chore rather than a rewarding journey.

Assessing and Reassessing Goals

Your goals may shift as you progress in your habit change journey. Regularly reassessing your goals ensures they remain aligned with your values and current life situation. This reassessment should involve reflecting on what you've achieved and what you now aspire to.

Introducing New Challenges

To keep the habit change process stimulating, introduce new challenges periodically. These challenges should stretch your abilities and push you out of your comfort zone, but still be achievable. This approach helps in maintaining a sense of excitement and accomplishment.

The Role of Feedback

Feedback is a valuable tool for adaptation. Seek feedback from yourself, through self-reflection, and from others, such as friends, family, or mentors. Use this feedback to make informed adjustments to your habit change strategies.

Learning from Setbacks

Setbacks are inevitable, but they also provide opportunities for learning and adaptation. Analyze what led to the setback and use these insights to refine your approach. This mindset turns challenges into valuable lessons.

Staying Informed

Staying informed about the latest research and developments in the field of habit change can provide new ideas and techniques to incorporate into your process. Whether it's a new app, a novel approach, or scientific insights, keep your knowledge up-to-date.

Experimentation

Don't be afraid to experiment with different strategies. What works for one person might not work for another, and what works at one stage of your journey might not be as effective later on. Experimentation keeps the process dynamic and personalized. While consistency is key in habit formation, incorporating variety prevents boredom. This could mean changing up your routine, setting different types of goals, or trying new methods to achieve your objectives.

Harnessing Technology

Technology can be a powerful ally in keeping your habit change process fresh. Use apps to track your progress, find online communities for support, or explore digital tools that offer new ways to approach habit change.

Mindful Evolution

As you evolve, so should your habits. Be mindful of how your needs, desires, and circumstances change over time. Your habit change process should reflect these evolutions, ensuring that it remains relevant and beneficial to your life.

Celebrating Adaptation

Celebrate not just your achievements but also your ability to adapt and evolve. This acknowledgment fosters a mindset that values growth and flexibility, which are essential in the ever-changing game of habit transformation.

A Dynamic Journey

In conclusion, keeping the habit change process fresh, adapting, and evolving is about embracing change as a constant and seeing each adaptation as a step forward in your journey. It's a dynamic process that requires creativity, flexibility, and a commitment to continual growth.

7. Engaging Friends and Family in Your Playful Habit Change

7.1 Building Your Team: Involving Loved Ones

Embarking on a journey of habit change is not a solitary endeavor. Involving loved ones can provide a supportive network, making the journey more manageable and enjoyable. This subchapter, drawn from extensive personal experience and insight, explores the importance of building your support team and effectively engaging friends and family in your habit change journey.

The Significance of a Support System

The role of a support system in habit change is multifaceted. It provides emotional encouragement, practical assistance, and accountability. Loved ones can act as cheerleaders, coaches, and teammates, offering support and motivation. Start by identifying who in your circle can serve as positive support. These individuals should be understanding, encouraging, and genuinely interested in your well-being. They can be family members, friends, colleagues, or even mentors.

Communicating Your Goals

Clear communication of your goals and reasons for change is crucial. Share with your support team what you are trying to achieve and why it is important to you. This clarity helps them understand your journey and how they can best support you.

Setting Boundaries and Expectations

Be clear about the type of support you need. Set boundaries and expectations to ensure that the support provided is helpful and not overwhelming or counterproductive. This could involve specifying how they can help, what kind of encouragement works for you, and how you wish to handle potential setbacks.

Involving Them in the Process

Find ways to involve your loved ones in your habit change process. This could include joint activities, regular check-ins, or shared goals. Involvement creates a sense of shared purpose and accountability.

The Role of Empathy and Understanding

Encourage empathy and understanding from your support team. They need to recognize that habit change is a challenging process, filled with highs and lows. Their empathy can provide comfort and reassurance during tough times.

Celebrating Together

Celebrate your successes with your support team. Sharing your victories not only makes the celebrations more joyful but also acknowledges their role in your journey. This shared revelry can strengthen relationships and provide mutual encouragement.

Handling Negative Influences

Be prepared to handle negative influences. Not everyone will be supportive or understand your journey. It's important to recognize who might be a hindrance to your progress and to manage these relationships carefully.

Building Mutual Respect

Foster a relationship of mutual respect with your support team. Respect their time and effort in supporting you and be appreciative of their involvement. Similarly, expect respect for your efforts and commitment to change.

Learning from Loved Ones

Be open to learning from your loved ones. They may offer valuable perspectives, advice, or strategies that can aid your habit change process. This openness can lead to unexpected insights and strengthen your approach to change.

The Impact of Shared Experiences

Shared experiences in habit change can lead to deeper connections with your loved ones. These shared journeys can be bonding experiences, fostering stronger relationships and a sense of communal achievement.

Conclusion: A Team Effort

In conclusion, building your team and involving loved ones in your habit change journey transforms the process from an individual challenge to a collective endeavor. It reinforces the idea that you are not alone in your journey, providing strength and support every step of the way.

7.2 Group Games: Collective Habit Changes

Embracing habit change as a collective journey can transform the process from a solitary struggle to an engaging group adventure. In this subchapter, I share insights on how group dynamics can be leveraged to facilitate collective habit changes, drawing from a wealth of personal experiences and observations.

The Power of Collective Action

The concept of changing habits in a group harnesses the power of collective action. This approach can amplify motivation, distribute the weight of challenges, and multiply the joy of success. It's about leveraging shared strength and commitment to achieve common goals.

Establishing Group Goals

Start by establishing clear, shared goals. These should be specific, measurable, and relevant to all group members. The process of setting these goals collectively ensures everyone is invested and on the same page.

Creating a Supportive Group Environment

Fostering a supportive group environment is essential. Encourage open communication, mutual respect, and empathy within the group. This positive atmosphere can significantly enhance motivation and perseverance.

Group Accountability

One of the key benefits of collective habit change is enhanced accountability. Set up systems where group members hold each other accountable, such as regular check-ins or progress reports. This accountability can be a powerful motivator and a source of encouragement.

Designing Group Challenges

Introduce group challenges that are fun, engaging, and suitable for all members. These could range from fitness challenges to group reading or meditation sessions. The key is to make these challenges enjoyable and inclusive.

Celebrating Group Achievements

Celebrate achievements as a group. Whether it's reaching a collective milestone or individual successes within the group, shared celebrations can strengthen the sense of community and shared purpose.

Leveraging Group Dynamics

Understand and leverage the dynamics of the group. Recognize the strengths and weaknesses of each member and how these can complement each other. This understanding can help in assigning roles and responsibilities that enhance the group's effectiveness.

Encouraging Peer Learning

Facilitate peer learning within the group. Encourage members to share their insights, strategies, and experiences. This exchange can be a rich source of learning and inspiration for all members.

Handling Conflicts

Be prepared to handle conflicts. Differences in opinions and approaches can arise in group settings. Address these conflicts constructively, focusing on open communication and finding common ground.

Adapting to Group Needs

Stay flexible and responsive to the changing needs of the group. Be open to adjusting goals, strategies, or structures to better suit the group's evolving dynamics and challenges.

Using Technology to Enhance Group Interaction

Utilize technology to enhance group interaction and coordination. Apps and online platforms can facilitate communication, tracking progress, and scheduling group activities.

The Ripple Effect of Collective Change

Collective habit change can have a ripple effect, extending beyond the group to influence families, communities, and broader networks. This wider impact can add a profound sense of purpose and significance to the group's efforts. Approaching habit change as a group game can transform the journey into an enriching and enjoyable experience. It's a testament to the idea that we are stronger together, capable of achieving remarkable transformations through collective effort and support.

7.3: The Power of Support and Encouragement

In the intricate dance of habit change, the role of support and encouragement from our social circle becomes a critical component of success. This subchapter, born from a lifetime of navigating personal transformations and supporting others in their journey, highlights the profound impact that support and encouragement can have on habit change.

Understanding the Value of Support

The journey of changing habits, often laden with challenges, can be significantly smoothed by the support of those around us. This support provides not just motivation but also a sense of accountability and belonging, key ingredients for long-term change.

Types of Supportive Actions

Support can come in various forms – emotional, practical, informational, and motivational. Emotional support includes empathy and understanding; practical support involves direct help; informational support offers advice and knowledge; and motivational support boosts morale and determination.

The Role of Encouragement

Encouragement acts as a catalyst in habit change. It's the positive reinforcement that keeps the momentum alive, especially during times of struggle or doubt. Encouragement can be as simple as a kind word, a gesture of acknowledgment, or sharing in the joy of small victories.

Building a Supportive Network

Cultivating a network of supportive individuals is crucial. This network can include family, friends, colleagues, or even online communities. The key is to surround yourself with people who believe in your ability to change and are invested in your success.

The Art of Asking for Support

Asking for support is an art that involves clear communication and vulnerability. It requires expressing your needs and goals while being open to receiving help. Remember, seeking support is not a sign of weakness but a strategic step in your habit change process.

Sharing Your Journey

Sharing your journey with your support network can strengthen the bond and enhance the support you receive. It involves being open about your challenges, progress, and insights. This transparency can foster deeper connections and understanding.

Giving Back: Supporting Others

Support is a two-way street. As you receive support, also look for opportunities to support others in their habit change efforts. This reciprocal approach can create a positive cycle of motivation and progress within your network.

The Impact of Positive Reinforcement

Positive reinforcement from your support network reinforces your efforts and achievements. Celebrating your progress, no matter how small, can provide a significant boost to your confidence and commitment.

Overcoming Negative Feedback

Not all feedback will be positive. Learning to deal with negative or unsupportive comments constructively is crucial. Focus on the constructive aspects of the feedback and use it as an opportunity to strengthen your resolve.

The Power of Role Models

Identifying role models within your support network can provide inspiration and a roadmap for your habit change journey. These are individuals who have achieved what you aspire to or who embody the principles of successful habit change.

Cultivating Gratitude

Expressing gratitude towards those who support and encourage you is vital. Gratitude not only acknowledges their role in your journey but also reinforces the positive dynamics of the supportive relationship.

The Strength in Togetherness

In conclusion, the power of support and encouragement in habit change cannot be overstated. It's about harnessing the strength found in togetherness, transforming the journey from a solitary endeavor to a shared adventure in growth and transformation.

8. CONCLUSION: TRIGGERING MASSIVE CHANGE WITH SMALL STEPS

8.1 The First Domino: Starting with Small Changes

Embarking on the journey of habit change often conjures images of monumental effort and drastic transformations. However, my life experience has taught me that massive change often starts with small, seemingly insignificant actions – the first domino in a chain of events leading to significant transformation. This subchapter delves into the power of small changes and how they can set the stage for substantial life alterations.

The Philosophy of Small Changes

Small changes are the manageable, bite-sized actions we can easily integrate into our daily routines. Their power lies not in their immediate impact, which may be subtle, but in their cumulative effect over time. Just like a small domino can topple much larger dominos in a chain, a small habit change can initiate a series of transformations. To appreciate the impact of small changes, it's crucial to understand their role in the broader context of habit formation and life transformation. These changes are like seeds planted today, which, with consistent care, grow into substantial results.

Setting Realistic and Achievable Goals

The key to successfully implementing small changes is to set realistic and achievable goals. These goals should be specific enough to be actionable yet small enough not to be overwhelming. For instance, starting with a five-minute meditation session each day is more feasible than aiming for an hour from the outset.

Building on Existing Habits

An effective strategy is to build small changes onto existing habits. Known as habit stacking, this involves adding a new habit to an already established one. For example, practicing gratitude right after brushing your teeth in the morning ensures the new habit piggybacks on the established one.

The Ripple Effect of Small Changes

Small changes often create a ripple effect, leading to more significant alterations in behavior and mindset. For instance, the simple act of organizing your workspace can lead to improved focus and productivity, which may then influence other areas of your work and personal life.

Overcoming Resistance with Small Steps

One of the biggest hurdles in habit change is resistance. Small changes are less intimidating and more manageable, making it easier to overcome this resistance. They act as the initial push needed to set change in motion.

Celebrating Small Victories

Recognizing and celebrating small victories is crucial. These celebrations reinforce the positive behavior and provide the motivation to continue. Each small victory is a step closer to your larger goal and deserves acknowledgment.

Tracking Progress

Keeping track of your progress, even the minor ones, can be incredibly motivating. It provides visual proof of how small changes accumulate over time, turning into significant achievements.

The Compound Effect of Small Changes

The compound effect is the principle that small, consistent actions add up to substantial results over time. Just like compound interest grows wealth, compound actions grow positive life changes. The key is consistency and time.

Adapting and Adjusting Small Changes

Be prepared to adapt and adjust your small changes as you progress. What starts as a small action may need to be expanded or modified as you grow and your needs change. Starting with small changes also offers psychological benefits. It builds confidence, reduces anxiety associated with change, and fosters a mindset of continuous improvement.

The First Domino: Initiating the Chain Reaction

The first small change is like pushing the first domino in a series. It initiates a chain reaction, where each small change builds upon the previous one, leading to a cascade of positive transformations. The journey of habit change need not be daunting. By focusing on small, manageable changes, you set in motion a process that can lead to significant life transformations. The first domino, once tipped, has the potential to topple many larger ones, leading to a path of continuous growth and improvement.

8.2 Momentum and Motivation: Keeping the Dominos Falling

In the intricate journey of habit change, maintaining the momentum of small steps to ensure continuous progress is crucial. This subchapter, enriched with a blend of personal experiences and expert insights, focuses on strategies to keep the dominos of habit change falling, thereby maintaining momentum and motivation throughout the process.

The Essence of Momentum in Habit Change

Momentum in habit change is akin to a domino effect – once initiated, each small success triggers the next, creating an ongoing cycle of positive change. The challenge lies in keeping this momentum alive, especially when obstacles arise or motivation wanes. Motivation is the fuel that keeps the dominos falling. However, it's not a constant resource and needs to be cultivated. Understanding the ebbs and flows of motivation and learning to reignite it when it diminishes is vital for sustained momentum.

The Role of Routine in Building Momentum

Establishing a routine around new habits is a powerful way to build momentum. Routines reduce the mental load of decision-making, turning desired behaviors into automatic actions that require less effort and thought as they become ingrained. Recognizing and celebrating progress, no matter how small, can significantly boost motivation. These celebrations serve as reminders of how far you've come and why you started, reinforcing your commitment to continue.

Using Visual Tools for Tracking Progress

Visual tools like charts, calendars, or apps that track progress can be highly effective. They provide a clear picture of your journey, showcasing each step forward, and help in maintaining focus on the ultimate goal. Plateaus and setbacks are an inevitable part of any change process. Developing visual strategies to overcome these challenges is crucial. This includes revisiting and possibly revising goals, trying new approaches, or seeking additional support.

The Impact of Social Support on Momentum

Social support can significantly influence momentum. Engaging with a community of like-minded individuals, finding an accountability partner, or simply sharing your journey with friends and family can provide encouragement and a renewed sense of purpose.

Harnessing the Power of Habit Stacking

Habit stacking, the process of adding new behaviors to established habits, can help maintain momentum. It simplifies the incorporation of new habits by associating them with existing routines, making it easier to sustain them over time.

Adjusting Goals as You Progress

As you make progress, your goals may need to be adjusted to reflect your new reality. This could mean setting higher targets, altering the direction of your efforts, or even adding new habits to continue your growth. While celebrating small victories, it's important to keep the end goal in sight. Regularly remind yourself of the bigger picture and how each small step is contributing to your larger objectives.

Staying Flexible and Adaptable

Flexibility and adaptability are key to maintaining momentum. Be open to changing your approach if certain strategies are no longer effective. Adaptability ensures that you keep moving forward, even if it means taking a different path.

Understanding the psychology behind small wins can be empowering. Each small win activates the reward system in the brain, releasing dopamine and creating a sense of pleasure and achievement, which in turn fuels further action.

Keeping the dominos falling in the habit change process is about nurturing a continuous journey of change. It involves a combination of consistent action, regular motivation, adaptability, and a deep understanding of the mechanisms that drive human behavior and change.

8.3 The Big Picture: Envisioning the Total Transformation

In the journey of habit change, it's crucial to occasionally step back and envision the broader transformation that these small changes are cultivating. This subchapter, drawing on a lifetime of personal growth and the wisdom gained from overcoming numerous challenges, delves into the art of visualizing the total transformation that can arise from a series of small, deliberate changes. Transformation is not just about altering a single habit; it's about a holistic change that affects various aspects of life. Envisioning this transformation requires an understanding of how small habits interconnect and influence our well-being, relationships, productivity, and overall life satisfaction.

The first step in envisioning your transformation is setting a clear and compelling vision. This vision should be inspiring, align with your core values, and reflect what you truly desire to achieve in your personal and professional life. A well-defined vision acts as a north star, guiding your daily actions and decisions. It helps maintain focus, especially when facing challenges or when motivation wanes. Your vision should be a constant reminder of why you started this journey. Creating a visual map of your transformation can be an effective tool. This could involve a vision board, a mind map, or a detailed written plan. The key is to make the envisioned transformation tangible and visible.

Engaging in regular visualization exercises can strengthen your commitment and belief in the transformation. Visualize not only the end result but also the process – the small steps you take each day that contribute to the big picture. Reflect on how this transformation could impact various areas of your life. Consider the potential improvements in health, relationships, career, and personal growth. Understanding these impacts can provide additional motivation. Ensure that your daily habits and actions are aligned with the big picture. Each habit should be a building block that contributes to the larger goal. Regular alignment checks can help keep you on track. While focusing on the big picture, it's important to embrace the journey. Transformation is not just about the destination; it's also about the growth and learning that occurs along the way.

Keeping the end vision in mind can help overcome challenges. When faced with obstacles, remind yourself of the transformation you're working towards and how each challenge is a stepping stone towards that goal. Incorporate your support system in your vision. Share your big picture with friends, family, or mentors. Their encouragement, feedback, and support can be vital in realizing your vision. Acknowledge and celebrate milestones along the way. These celebrations should honor the progress made towards the larger transformation, reinforcing the positive changes and keeping the vision alive. Be open to adjusting your vision as you evolve. Transformation is dynamic, and your vision may need refinement as you gain new insights, experiences, and understanding of what you truly want. Envisioning the total transformation as a result of small habit changes offers a comprehensive perspective on the journey of personal development. It's about seeing beyond the immediate horizon to the grand landscape of change that lies ahead, filled with potential and promise.

A Personal Note from the Author

If you enjoyed reading this book, I would be incredibly grateful if you could take a moment to share your thoughts with a review. Your feedback not only helps me, but it also assists fellow readers in discovering this book. Thank you for your support!

Ralph Sterling

www.ingramcontent.com/pod-product-compliance
Lightning Source LLC
LaVergne TN
LVHW012127070526
838202LV00056B/5894